COMMON THINGS

WHICH OUGHT TO BE MADE

Universally Known.

ROYSTON: JOHN WARREN.

M.DCCC.LXXX.

PREFACE.

A PREFACE to these letters on " Common Things "
can be only a postscript; or rather it may be suggested that the two first letters of the series might
be permitted to serve as a preface to the later
written letters, which were added, some years subsequently, in order that the subject, submitted to
consideration in the two first letters, might be treated
in some measure of completeness.

Three principal objects are proposed to be aimed
at in these letters.

I. The placing, in its *proper* position, of the
Profession of Medicine and Surgery.

II. The rescue of our countrymen and women
from the degradation arising from indulgence in
intemperance.

III. The rescue of our countrymen and youths from the degradation arising from the *chewing* and smoking of tobacco.*

I. With reference to the *first* of these objects— may it not be said that the grand *Opprobrium Medicinæ*, or reproach of Medicine, consists—

> (*a*) in the fact, that the Profession of Medicine and Surgery still continues to demean itself by accepting *fees* instead of a *salary* ?

> (*b*) in the fact, that the Profession does not lay claim to that which ought to be its right, namely, its right to have full power to avert diseases and accidents, by means of fore-thought, foresight, and all practicable pro-vision, against diseases and accidents ?

II. With reference to the *second* of these objects— may it not be said that to the peculiar severity of the climate of our native land must *mainly* be attributed the *over*-devotion of our people to the imbibing of intoxicating liquors ?

III. With reference to the *third* of these objects— may it not be said that to the same peculiar severity of our climate must *mainly* be attributed the abandon-ment of our men to the *chewing* and smoking of tobacco ?

---

* After nearly 300 years, since the "Counter-blast to Tobacco," of Bonnie King James's time, may not the hope be entertained that the gentle influence of the more highly favoured sex will, sooner or later, bring about the removal of that *exceptional* disgrace to the human race, the use of tobacco —a disgrace which the tribes of Apes and Baboons do not share with it !

Holding a cigar between the lips—is *that* anything less than a *mild* method of *chewing* tobacco leaves?

About the year 1840, an accident first drew my attention to the fact that Doctors held a power in their hands which they did not so fully make use of as they ought to do.

Having a cold, attended with hoarseness, I was cured, in a short time, by taking a Mixture prescribed for me by the late Dr. James Copland (the compiler of the Dictionary of Medicine). This Mixture I have ventured to call "Camphor Julep"; the prescription is given in the first of these letters. But Dr. Copland never told me that, by taking a little of this "Camphor Julep" *in time*, the ill-effects of a cold could be prevented; he left me to find *that* out for myself. And having made this discovery, I have, for many years, done what I could to promulgate this useful piece of knowledge. Had the value of this Mixture been *made universally known*, as it ought to have been, many years since, millions of lives (which have come to an untimely end) might have been lengthened; and millions on millions of hours of tedious and tormenting illness and suffering from affections innumerable of the throat and of the lungs might have been spared by the *timely* use of "Camphor Julep." It is supposed very generally that "smoking an early pipe," or taking "a drop of rum and milk," or some other strong drink, will prevent the catching of colds, coughs, fevers, &c.; but it is not so well known as it ought to be that taking half a wine-glassful of "Camphor Julep" — about one half-penny worth—will protect the throat, from the attacks of such diseases, better than smoking, and drinking all the strong or warm drinks in the world.

Earlsbury Park,   HENRY CLINTON.
Barkway, near Royston, Herts.,
17th Jan., 1880.

ONE OF THE "COMMON THINGS" WHICH OUGHT TO BE UNIVERSALLY MADE KNOWN.

No. 1.

From the EASTERN POST, *January 20th,* 1872.

TO THE EDITOR.

SIR,—During every hour of every day, and during every hour of every night, somewhere in the world, millions of persons are *suffering* from complaints of the Throat, and of the Chest; at every instant in the day, and at every instant in the night, somewhere in the world, one poor human creature is *dying* of Bronchitis, of Laryngitis, of Consumption, of Diphtheria, or of some other affection of the Throat, or of the Lungs, having its origin in the Throat; and many of all these individuals are thus suffering excruciating torments, and many are dying, *solely* because some members of the Medical Profession, omit, or neglect, the performance of *that* which must be considered one of their chief duties, the duty, namely, of *preventing* such disease, such suffering, and such death.

Sometime before the year 1840, the late Dr. James Copland gave me the Prescription for Camphor Julep—below mentioned—in order to *cure* a hoarseness.

Having once experienced the usefulness of this Prescription, it occurred to me, that many affections of the Throat, and of the Lungs, might be *prevented*, or *averted*, by having *timely* recourse to the use of this Prescription.

This I found to be really so—and, now, after the experience of so many (upwards of thirty) years, I may perhaps be permitted to assert that the never-failing efficacy of this Prescription, in *preventing*, as well as in *alleviating*, and in *curing* many complaints of the Throat, and of the Lungs, has been quite satisfactorily proved.

Under this conviction, I have, from time to time, attempted to engage Members of the Medical Profession to place alongside of this Prescription something just as efficacious, but simpler, and less costly, so that it might always be within the reach of, even, the poorest persons, who might happen to stand in need of having recourse to it. But I have, invariably, been met with the *assurance that it is not possible to prevent disease.*

It is needless to say that, in the face of all these authorities, I, for my part, (prompted by my own long experience, and by the experience of numerous persons, who have received, from time to time, the greatest benefit from the use of this prescription,) have not the slightest remains of faith in any such *assurance;* and it is impossible to overlook this fact, namely, that, if the statements of the said authorities are trustworthy, the *best* possible thing to bring "grist" to the Professional Profit-Mill happens to coincide very remarkably, with the *worst* possible thing for the welfare of the whole human race.

In defiance, then, of the *assurance* of all those members of the Medical Profession who still declare that disease cannot be prevented, I wish to make this fact generally known, viz., that many diseases which originate, or which have their seat in the throat, and in the respiratory organs, will be prevented, or removed (or the sufferings arising from them will be greatly alleviated) by the *timely* use of Camphor Julep.

This medicine is no new discovery, but the merits of it (especially as a *preventive*) seem to have been, too long, sadly overlooked.

Without its *Doctor's Latin* Dress the Prescription is as follows :—

Camphor Water.........Four ounces.
Spirit of Minderer......One and a quarter ounce.
Sweet Spirit of Nitre...Half an ounce.
Ipecacuanha Wine......One quarter of an ounce.
Simple Syrup ....Two ounces.

The measures are in fluid ounces.

"These ingredients form a mixture which may be denominated a COLD and COUGH MIXTURE, or a THROAT and CHEST ELIXIR."*

If people wish to protect the Throat, and the Lungs, from diseases of many kinds, let them take

---

* These were the words of Dr. Copland. I have ventured to suggest the name of CAMPHOR JULEP.

one, two, three, or four, teaspoonfuls of this Camphor Julep, as often as any feeling of uneasiness in the throat occurs; and, *as a safeguard* to the throat, and to the lungs, *during the night*, especially, let them take one teaspoonful of it the *last thing at night*.

Long experience induces me to believe that even one teaspoonful of this Camphor Julep, *taken in time*, will often suffice to keep the throat, and the lungs, safe from the attacks of disease for a more or less extended period of time.

Earlsbury Park,   HENRY CLINTON.
  near Royston, Herts.,
   Jan. 19th, 1872.

ROYSTON PRESS: JOHN WARREN.

ONE OF THE "COMMON THINGS" WHICH OUGHT TO BE UNIVERSALLY MADE KNOWN.

No. 2.

From the EASTERN POST, *March 4th,* 1872.

TO THE EDITOR.

SIR,—Your kind indulgence having allowed me space in your columns (in the *Eastern Post* of the 20th and 21st of January) for the purpose of showing how, by taking care to keep the *throat* in a healthy state, a very important part of the *upper* region of the body may be, to a great extent, protected from Disease, I now venture to request you to permit me to make a brief statement with respect to the simple means, nearest at hand, by which the *lower* region of the body, likewise, may be considerably protected from liability to attacks of Diseases of many kinds.

There are thousands of persons who seldom need to have recourse to the very simple preventive means which I mention ; and no one ought to take medicine of any sort, as a preventive, unless there should be indications pointing to the probability that having *timely* recourse to such preventive means may serve to ward off the beginning of Disease.

This is premised, equally, with reference to the measures suggested with the view of *internally* protecting both the *upper* and the *lower* regions of the body.

It can hardly be necessary to state that, of course, *proper* Temperance, and proper regard for the best known methods of regulating Diet must always be the mainstays for securing the healthy condition of the human body.

But—next after these chief matters for consideration—may it not be assumed that the *first* general law, which must be laid down, is *that* law which insists upon the expediency of giving timely, and proper, aid to nature (whenever such aid seems to be needed) in keeping, as far as possible, the whole length of the internal passages of the body clear from obstructions of whatsoever kind?

Such obstructions may be distinguished as :

I. Obstructions occurring in the *Throat*.

II. Obstructions occurring in the *Intestines*.

With reference to obstructions in the *Throat*— viz., from Phlegm (the *mala pituita* of the Romans), and from other affections in the throat—I will say no more, here, than that the *Eastern Post* of the 20th and 21st of January last gave a full account of the very simple means by which, on almost all occasions, the *Throat* may be kept in a healthy state—such healthy state of the *Throat* serving, in great measure, to secure the Larynx, the Bronchial Tubes, and the Lungs, from *external* attacks of Disease.

With reference to obstructions in the *Intestines* it must be said that, without the advice of the Medical Profession, very little can, safely, be undertaken in the way of preventing Diseases which are liable to be occasioned by such obstructions.

Shall I lay myself open to blame if I venture to assert that the *timely*, and proper, taking of, even, a "Seidlitz Powder," the *first thing in the morning*— occasionally—whenever (and *only* when) it seems to be required, might prevent such obstructions in almost innumerable instances, and thus serve to avert an infinite amount of suffering from *Disease*, and an incalculable number of premature *Deaths?*

It is hardly necessary to say that no one ought ever to take even a "Seidlitz Powder," unless one has reason to believe that one ought to do so.

"Experientia *docet*"—the old saying may be paraphrased, in translating, thus :

Experience teaches us, at last, how many nauseous *doses* we might have, very well, done without.

In self-defence, and in deprecation of all the reproaches apparently merited by the presumption with which I have, so far, ventured to lay before the public the results of my own experience, in these matters, I must be permitted to add that I should not have come forward, in this way, if I had ever had the good fortune to meet with one member of the Medical Profession who had shown that he possessed the *moral courage* requisite to enable him to give such a plain statement, on the subject, as the foregoing.

And I venture, still farther, to say this—viz. :

That which *ought* to be done, *must* be done, and

must be done as speedily as possible, to relieve the
noblest of the Professions (the Medical Profession)
from the oppressive weight of that mysterious
Incubus which seems, hitherto, to have deterred *too
many* of the members of that Profession from rendering, to their poor fellow-mortals the full advantages
of the undoubted power which the Profession holds
in its hands, namely, the power of saving life—the
power of averting, and of preventing suffering from
Disease, and of postponing the triumph of eventually
inevitable death.

Earlsbury Park,   HENRY CLINTON.
nr. Royston, Herts.,
24th Feb., 1872.

ROYSTON PRESS: JOHN WARREN.

ONE OF THE

"COMMON THINGS"

WHICH

OUGHT TO BE

UNIVERSALLY

MADE KNOWN.

No. 3.

ONE OF THE COMMON THINGS WHICH OUGHT TO BE UNIVERSALLY MADE KNOWN.

No 3.

The mysterious *Incubus* to which I referred in my letter, No. 2, published in "The Eastern Post" of the 4th of March, 1872, as acting oppressively, and perniciously, by its burthen, upon the Profession of Medicine ought, surely, to be no mystery at all, *now*, to anybody. *That* Incubus is the Self-Interest of the "Doctors."

The Medical *Profession*, as at present constituted, is a *trade*. Now, every one knows the meaning of the expression—"It is all for the good of trade." Nobody, thèn, can doubt that people who trade must contrive, somehow or other, to live by their trade.

This being so — the more ill-health there may happen to be at any time, in any locality, the more demand is there for the services of "doctors," the greater the run upon the establishments of chemists and druggists, of undertakers, &c. Inwardly, then, "doctors," and chemists must, more or less, look forward to improved trade, whenever, and wherever, accidents, fevers, epidemics, or ill-health generally are to be found.

Is *this*, really, the fact, or is it not the fact? If it *is* the fact, is not such a condition of things most deplorable? But, then, there must be a remedy for such a terrible state of things. Now, what *is* the remedy? It is a very simple one.

Medical attendants must be remunerated by *salaries*, paid by government, *not* by *fees*, paid by patients. A sufficient number of physicians, and surgeons, and dispensers of medicine, and nurses, must be appointed *by government* in every locality, with due regard to the amount, and to the "density," of the population, and to the greater, or less, superficial area in which the population of each locality dwells. A sufficient sum must be set apart from the annual revenue of the nation, for the adequately liberal remuneration, by salary, for the services rendered by all persons so appointed. The system of fee-charging, and of fee-taking, by medical officials, must cease—*gradually*—*pari passu*—accordingly as a sufficient number of persons can be found competent to undertake the performance of the duties of various offices to which they may be appointed by government.

To the "Cabinet" of Ministers must be added a Secretary of State of the Sanitary, (or Medical,) department, with whom, assisted by a council of Emeriti-Surgeons, and Physicians, would rest all appointments to medical office.

When it is considered what an enormous sum of money is lavished, year by year, upon, so-called, "religion," and upon "education," no one, surely, could be found so unreasonable as to grudge the setting apart of a sufficient portion of the national revenue for the *comfortable* establishment of a really serviceable body of medical attendants.

"Doctors" ought to be appointed to the cure of *bodies*, in like manner, as clergymen, for a thousand years, have been appointed to the cure of *souls*, in parishes. Were this done, *judiciously*-selected "Doctors," having before them the certainty that *fairly* - adequate remuneration for life-long service, in their professional duty, was to be assured to them, would eagerly vie with their *Reverend Parishonal Colleagues*, and would, doubtless, in *their own* cure of *bodies*, manifest, zeal and success, at least, equal to those of their reverend and "spiritual" brethren, in *their* cure of *souls*.

It is very necessary to ask the question why soldiers, and sailors, and their officers, their wives, and their families, why the inmates of Union Workhouses, and of Gaols, &c., are privileged to enjoy the advantage of having their health cared for, *free of cost*, while all the rest of the world are left to the "tender mercies" of *amateur*—because *uncovenanted*—physicians, and surgeons, apothecaries, chemists and druggists, &c. ?

"A spade must be called a spade"—while, at the same time, to "the Devil" must be presented "his due." The members of the medical and surgical profession form, in the main, a most intelligent, enlightened, even illustrious body ; and, whenever that body shall have shaken off the above-mentioned *Incubus* of Self-Interest, there can be no doubt that any possible improvement of which it may be found capable will follow, as surely as the day succeeds the night.

There is, however, one objection which may be raised to the manner in which—if doctors can be said to have any *express* duties at all towards their patients, or customers—such duties are performed by them.

The most ignorant person in the world must feel that almost all the diseases which afflict mortals are chiefly owing to either accident, or to ignorance of their own, or to remissness, on their part, in not having applied, *in time*, to their " doctor," in order that the access of disease might be averted. The human body is a tragi-comical chemical machine, which needs, almost continually, *sufficient* looking after, if it is to be kept in good order. It may be said that, if every individual could secure, and follow, *in time*, the advice of his " doctor," *comparatively* little ill-health would have to be suffered from, by the mass of mankind.

The *retaining* of good health, by averting an attack of disease, *of any kind*, or by preventing, at an early stage of it, the continuance of such an attack, is, comparatively speaking, an easy matter, but one which requires constant attention, and due precaution.

On the other hand, too easy is the path leading *down the hill* to bad health ; whilst the return to good health is too frequently, terribly " *up-hill* " work, and out of all proportion more difficult.

In these two respects the words of Virgil, on a very different subject, are applicable.

Facilis descensus Averno :
Noctes atque dies patet atri janua Ditis :
Sed revocare gradum, superasque evadere ad auras,
Hoc opus, hic labor est.

Thus far—the " Doctor," and the Philanthropist, may, possibly, proceed together, hand in hand, in some degree, amicably ; but here, at *this* point, the " Doctor" will, certainly, start away, " at a tangent," and will denounce the threatened interference of the Philanthropist, who, in the name, and in behalf, of humanity, would fain see the " Doctor " relieved from the *excess* of " labour, and of work," which the " Doctor's " *benevolence* secures to himself, because he refrains from establishing a proper system of preventing the attacks of disease.

Earlsbury Park,   HENRY CLINTON.
near Royston, Herts.,
21st April, 1879.

ROYSTON PRESS: JOHN WARREN.

ONE OF THE

"COMMON THINGS"

WHICH

OUGHT TO BE

UNIVERSALLY

MADE KNOWN.

No. 4.

ONE OF THE COMMON THINGS WHICH OUGHT TO BE UNIVERSALLY MADE KNOWN.

No. 4.

"There is no armour against Fate;
Death lays his icy hands on kings:
  Sceptre and Crown
  Must tumble down,
And in the dust, be equal made
With the poor crooked scythe and spade."
"Golden lads, and girls, all must
Like chimney-sweepers come to dust."

Verily is there no armour against *eventual* Fate—that is against Death—but that which may be be called *premature* Death may be postponed, or deferred, for a more or less protracted period, or term of years, by taking *timely* precaution, or by the aid of a *disinterested* "doctor."

Kinsmen, and kinswomen, of mine (more or less distantly related to my family), the late Lord and Lady Amberley,—who died a year or two since,—Princess Alice, the daughter of the Queen of England, and Prince Waldemar of Prussia, the grandson of the Queen, who both died recently—might all have been alive at this time, had they known, and had they availed themselves of the knowledge, that a teaspoonful of "camphor julep,"* *taken in time*, would have prevented the attack of diphtheria from which it has been their unhappy fate, *prematurely*, to die—because of their own ignorance, and because of the ignorance on the part of their medical attendants, in regard to the marvellously protective powers of "camphor julep."

For many years—indeed, ever since I have known the efficacy of "camphor julep" in averting diseases of many kinds from the throat, and from the lungs—I have endeavoured to obtain the aid of "doctors" in promulgating the fact. And what has been my success in those endeavours? One gentleman said, "Oh! you know that we must expect 'colds' at this season of the year." Another person asked me—"if I did not believe that 'colds' were ordained to come for our good?" No doubt!—"Just as a cold may prove beneficial to the doctor's trade, whilst it results in death to the patient." One highly distinguished physician, a most liberal-minded gentle-

---

* CAMPHOR JULEP. (The late Dr. James Copland's.)
  4ozs. of Camphor Water,
  1½oz. of Spirit of Mindererus.
  ½oz. of Sweet Spirit of Nitre,
  ½oz. of Ipecacuanha Wine,
  2ozs. of Simple Syrup.

man, met my repeated earnest entreaty that he would bear public testimony to the value of " camphor julep," as preventing consumption and other diseases (of the throat), with the reply that " consumption and other diseases came on from various causes. That, in such cases, physicians had much to do, and that no one remedy could do much." Another highly distinguished physician silenced me by saying that he did not like " amateur-doctoring " — quite forgetting, the while, how little better than an " amateur-doctor " he was himself, with all his knowledge and all his vast experience. The same gentleman has since admitted in writing that " camphor julep " is indeed " a valuable medicine, and one that would not easily kill any person." Another doctor in the *Eastern Post* (March, 1872) decried this " camphor julep " of Dr. Copland as " a harmless saline mixture " — a mere " chip in porridge," a " broken reed to depend on against catarrh." To this I would observe that " camphor julep " must not be regarded as a curative or as a preventive of catarrh, but as the most efficacious means (hitherto known) of averting *from the throat* the evil consequences of an attack of catarrh (in plain English a " common cold "). A celebrated chemist asked me— whence I had got that " hodge-podge ?" Even Dr. Copland, who conferred upon me the signal benefit of the knowledge of this life-saving Elixir — even that eminent gentleman did not give it to me as a *preventive* to affections of the throat, and of the lungs ; he left me to find *that* out by experience ; possibly he did not, himself, know the full degree of marvellously protecting power possessed by the very prescription which he wrote for me. In fact, is it not clear that if human beings are to be *properly* attended to *in* health and *out* of health, in life and in death, the self-interest of doctors, as well as of certain other persons, must be enlisted on the side of humanity, which can hardly be said to be the case at the present time.

The Professions of " Doctors " and " Lawyers " have hitherto monopolised to themselves the title of the " Liberal " Professions—but is not this a confounding of terms ? The only Professions which can ever claim a right to bear that designation are the Professions of which the Members make a " covenant " with a public authority to undertake to perform certain duties, on condition of receiving an annual salary, by quarterly, or yearly payments, in return for the performance of the respective duties *covenanted* by them to be *so* performed in each Profession.

The soldier, the sailor, and the Civil Government official, even the labourer working for fixed weekly wages, might be honoured as belonging to a "liberal" Profession, rather than "Doctors" and "Lawyers"—for a soldier does not bargain for a fee every time he takes the post of sentinel; the sailor does not bargain for a fee every time he joins the watch on deck; the civilian official does not bargain for a fee every time he takes his place at the office desk. Why, then, should the "Doctor," and the "Lawyer," be allowed to call their Professions *par excellence* "Liberal," without having demonstrated their patriotism by openly, and formally, undertaking certain *covenanted* duties, in like manner, as their fellow-citizens in other before-mentioned Professions have done?

In short — the two Professions, which have hitherto, by some confusion of ideas, been nicknamed "Liberal," are the two, especially, *illiberal*, and extortionate Professions, and, as such, they are to be denounced, and they ought to be brought under proper control, in behalf of their sorely oppressed, and down-trodden fellow-creatures.

If we wish to secure for ourselves good *health* at the least possible cost, and *justice* at the least possible cost—the members of these two, so called, Liberal Professions must become *covenanted* officials of our Government. Each "doctor" must be *under covenant* to the Government to do his utmost to keep in health everybody whom he has under his charge in the parish, or district, to which he shall have been appointed; while each "Lawyer" (whether barrister or attorney) must be under covenant to the Government to do his utmost to prevent injustice being suffered by any person whom he has under his charge in the parish or district to which he shall have been appointed.

The "Doctor"—who would, *knowingly*, injure, instead of securing, the good health of a patient—has his fitting counterpart in his brother of that other so called "Liberal" Profession, the "Lawyer" —that man, namely, who, *knowingly*, undertakes to advocate the cause of *injustice*, on the part of his own client, versus the cause of *justice*, claimed by the other side—and either of these—*(par nobile fratrum)* —viz., such a "Doctor," or such a "Lawyer," would equally deserve the honour of being termed one of the "Devil's own Advocates."

Earlsbury Park,   HENRY CLINTON.
near Royston, Herts.,
5th May, 1879.

ROYSTON PRESS: JOHN WARREN.

ONE OF THE "COMMON THINGS" WHICH OUGHT TO BE UNIVERSALLY MADE KNOWN.

No. 5.

People calling themselves Christians have, hitherto, for many a year, joined, more or less thoughtlessly, in the burden of the old ditty :

> I care for nobody, no, not I—
> If nobody cares for me.

This sentiment chimes in very well with the proverbial dictum—

> Everyone for himself—and God for us all.

In other words—"The Devil take the hindmost" in the race for a "competency," if not for a "fortune."

But would it not be doing the antecedents of our race injustice to say that such a sentiment, as the above, was scarcely worthy of the *pre*-Christian world ?

With a slight change, and perhaps, not without some injury to the *rhythm*, but with some improvement to the (so-called Christian) *reason* contained in the sentiment of the ditty above, I have for many years felt that the burden of that song might well be reversed thus :

> And this the burden of his song,
> For ever it used to be—
> I will care for the whole world, that will I,
> Though no one may care for me.

And it is in behalf of humanity that I write this letter, No. 5, on this 16th of June, 1879. But, on *this very morning*, I meet with statements, purporting to have been made, by Mr. W. E. Gladstone, at the "Savage" Club Dinner, on Saturday last—statements which tend greatly to cause me to despair of being able to effect any good whatever in proceeding with this letter. I will quote those statements.

Mr. Gladstone complained that "all the work that we have to do in a political sphere is the roughest that man can conceive. He loses the edge of his finer faculties—faculties demoralised by politics."

This statement would make it appear as if there must be considerable blame chargeable against the *sort* of politics favoured by the Rt. Hon. gentleman. For, surely, the prime questions of the *right sort* of politics ought to tend to the refining of the finer faculties, rather than to the blunting of their edge. As an instance—the study of "Political Economy" must, surely, constitute some small part, at least, of politics ; and political economy, it can scarcely be denied, ought to have its finest faculties sharpened, and polished up, to the highest degree, if it sets itself to the task of effecting the utmost possible good for all. I have, elsewhere, stated :

"Foresight must regulate all : what *can* be arranged in advance ·
Must wisely be *ordered*, not left to caprice or to chance."
"Let us earnestly work, for the task is not small
Of providing for *comfort* to *each* by providing for *justice* to *all*."

Again, the Rt. Hon. Gentleman said : " But, Gentlemen, I am a free trader. I love not the spirit of monopoly."

Again, the Rt. Hon. Gentleman said : " It is a pleasure to think that commerce, and manufacture, and even law, and sometimes medicine, can offer to their votaries the means of creating fortunes which they can hand down honourably to their descendants, and that even literature has not been shut out from that privilege."

Such statements as these falling from the eloquent lips of the Rt. Hon. Gentleman, I say, make me almost despair of succeeding in my endeavours to persuade the world how good and wholesome a thing it would be if " doctors," nurses, and " undertakers " were *covenanted* to, and *appointed* by, Government, and *paid salaries* by Government, respectively, in remuneration for the services which they perform.

Observe—that the Rt. Hon. Gentleman " loves not monopoly," yet has "pleasure to think that" *an exceedingly minute portion*, of the whole population of the globe—of the thousand millions of its, more or less, wretched inhabitants—" has not been shut out from the *privilege* of creating fortunes which they can hand down honourably to their descendants."

But before we arrive at contemplating the pleasure of seeing those fortunes handed down honourably to descendants, are we not impelled to ask the very important question — Have these fortunes been *created* honourably ? Fortunes which *have* been *created honourably* may, without any doubt, be *handed down* honourably to descendants, but, of all the fortunes which have ever been made, how many can be said to have been *created* honourably ?

Fortunes are *inherited;* fortunes are *acquired* through wealthy marriages ; but, for the most part, fortunes can be *created*, in any possible business, in only one or two ways.

I. By giving less than a fair share of remuneration for service performed ; or—

II. By retaining in your hands more than a fair share of the price of goods which you distribute.

And how much honour can accrue to any one in *creating* fortunes through such means?

Just 20 years since, in the year 1859, I published a short paper which demonstrated the iniquity of the system which permits fortunes to be *thus* created, and with which system Mr. Gladstone appears to be so thoroughly well satisfied.

In "*The Screw Loose in the Machinery of Society,*" it was stated that "a considerable number of persons, belonging to every branch of society, are no longer permitted, (as they were in former times,) to take to themselves inordinate profits in the course of the performance of *their duty* towards society." This being so, why should *any members* of any of the branches of society be permitted to reserve for themselves exorbitant profits, in the course of the performance of *their duty* towards society? Is not there consummate foolishness in suffering such iniquity to continue? For all the members of all the branches of society are all *alike producers—providers* (in one way or other) of *comfort—contributors* (each in *her*, or in *his*, own way) towards the establishment of the *well-being* of society in general; for they *undertake* to *provide* for *comfort*, respectively, by affording *protection* thus (in *alphabetical* order) :—

1. The *Civilian*......protects from discomfort generally
2. The "*Doctor*" ...protects from ill-health ;
3. The *Lawyer* ......protects from injustice ;
4. The *Merchant* ...protects from extortion in demand ;
5. The *Producer* ...protects from deficient supply ;
6. The *Sailor*.........protects from War by *sea*, &c. ;
7. The *Soldier* ......protects from War by *land*, &c. ;
8. The *Teacher* ......protects from ignorance.

And of all these branches of society, some members of the 1st, 2nd, 3rd, 4th, 5th, and 8th branches, do, from time to time, create fortunes—whilst the members of the 6th and 7th branches have very seldom, if ever, a chance of creating a fortune which they can hand down, either honourably, or dishonourably, to their descendants.

"All the members of each of these branches of society ought to be looked upon as performing (each in their own department) a *public duty*, of more or less importance, towards society, inasmuch as they are all, alike, producers of comfort—all, alike, purveyors of the protection required by the needs of society against *dis*comfort of all kinds.

"Now—regard of *justice* demands that *all* the members of *all* these branches of society, according to a definite scale of compensation—shall be remunerated, in return for the *public duty* which they, *themselves*, respectively, perform, for any *unavoidable* loss of time in performing that duty, and for any employment of *capital of their own*, and of *skill of their own* in their respective occupations.

"Is it not the *duty* of society to see, as *far as possible*, that, in the allotment of such compensation, each individual producer of each article tending to the general comfort of all society, shall be treated as *fairly as possible*?

"Now—common-sense informs us that this *duty* can never be done, unless *whatever* can be considered as the legitimate *business* of public barter and sale shall have been taken out of the hands of *private* individuals, and shall be carried on by the officials of society, *in each district*, at the cost price of economical and yet liberal management, for the benefit of society.

"Has not, from the earliest to the latest periods of society, a most enormous amount of *discomfort* to the world had its origin in the deficiency of public arrangements for securing, *as far as possible*, the payment of *fair* compensation for labour (or service of any kind) performed by each, and every member of all the branches of society? It seems to me not right that the *main body* of the members of all the branches of society should, for any longer time, be left to *scramble* for their *rights* in this matter.

"'Prevention is better than Cure.' The *best* justice is *injustice prevented*.—Protection from injustice.—In this matter, it appears to me, that 'Political Economists' have committed their grossest sin, one of omission; in as far as they have ignored, altogether, the *duty* of society towards its members."

After somewhat of a digression, I return to the consideration of the question whether human beings are, really, properly attended to in health, or in sickness, in life, or in death? The question suggested itself to my mind as I was thinking on the three trades followed by the "doctors," the nurses, and the "undertakers," respectively.

Weird as the designation of the last avocation may seem on the surface, I, for one, do not necessarily imply in the term of "undertaker" any unpleasant association of ideas; for are we not all of us undertakers in a less restricted sense of the word? all those of us who have to "*undertake*" to perform some duty or duties towards society?

Earlsbury Park,   HENRY CLINTON.
near Royston, Herts.,
16th June, 1879.

ONE OF THE "COMMON THINGS" WHICH OUGHT TO BE UNIVERSALLY MADE KNOWN.

No. 6.

In my last letter, No. 5, I pointed out that the "doctor" undertakes (or that he ought to do so)—as far as human zeal and power go—to protect society from ill-health. I now wish to add to this that the nurse acts (or ought to act) as the *sine qua non* secondary in the "doctor's" undertakings ; whilst the "undertaker"—the "undertaker" colloquially so called—enters upon the scene when life has become extinct. *Then* it is that *he* undertakes to perform his solemn duties to the dead most conscientiously on his part, and with a delicate regard for the natural feelings of the mourners—be they relatives or friends.

Now, as many persons will be inclined to agree with me, a very large proportion of our "doctors," nurses, and "undertakers," *may be* skilful and likewise conscientious, in carrying out their respective undertakings. But *may be* is nothing more than a "*skin-deep*" probability. As with so many other arrangements left to take care of themselves, what guarantees, what security has society that such undertakings *shall be* honestly carried out? I say, none whatever. For no measures have ever been taken or framed for well defining the duties and obligations of the three categories of "undertakers" which have been described above.

And with regard to the respective merits or demerits of these attendants, it is simply left to customers themselves to find them out, and that, moreover, on the most unsatisfactory *data*.

The "doctor" and the nurse, alike, ought to be held responsible, in a sense, for the treatment, the health and the comfort of those whom they have undertaken to attend. And, as far as his trade is concerned, suitable responsibility should be made to rest upon the shoulders of the "undertaker."

Persons engaged in these three businesses, "doctors," nurses, and "undertakers" ought to form one corporate body; and I submit that every individual belonging to that body, when formed, ought to be looked upon, in their several respective offices, as servants of the Government.

There is no possibility of *making sure* that these people should act conscientiously, in the performance of their official duties, even according to their own *private* notions of conscientiousness ; but a *public* "*standard*" of conscientiousness, in discharging their *defined* duties towards their customers *might* be established ; and I venture to maintain that such a "standard" ought to be established by whatever means which society may find that it has the power to exert in securing the establishment of such a "standard," and in the steadfast upholding of the same, to the manifest advantage of the whole community.

The task which I find before me, in closing my treatment of this subject is a very irksome and, even, a most revolting one, to me, viz., that of briefly showing cause for a total change in the system of remunerating the services of "doctors," of nurses, and of "undertakers."

Giving all the credit, which may be due, and which *is*, undoubtedly, due in very many cases, to a large proportion of persons engaged in these three occupations, for a more or less conscientious performance of duties towards those on whom they attend, it can hardly be required that many details should be entered into with reference to complaints of various defects and deficiencies, and to charges of, even, the very grossest criminality, to which, as human creatures, persons engaged in these three businesses are, unhappily, too liable.

Volumes upon volumes might be written, if details were demanded, on the subject of the defects, of the shortcomings, of the negligences, of the crimes, even, with which too many persons, working in these "businesses," not to call them *all* by the same term—"trades"—have, from time to time, been chargeable.

They best can paint them who have felt them most.

But, speaking generally, where can there be found one individual who has not to relate some sad experience, the result of unskilfulness, or ignorance, carelessness, or criminality on the part of some person engaged on these employments ?

In the case of "*doctors*" the greatest skill, with high honour, and with *uncommon* honesty is absolutely required.

In the case of nurses great skill with honour, and with *uncommon* honesty, is, also, absolutely required.

In the case of "undertakers" no skill whatever is required, but honour, and *un*common honesty indeed.

What more need be said? I consider it only necessary to mention one or two instances, (and those by no means the worst cases in each category,) which go a good way towards proving that "doctors," nurses, and "undertakers" ought to be officials, *covenanted to the public service*, and that such officials ought *only* to be appointed, and admitted to such offices when their conscientious behaviour in such offices can be *guaranteed*.

I. A specimen of a " *doctor*."

A gentleman of very moderate means, over sixty years of age, was, a few years since, persuaded, in an unlucky hour, by the governor of a large public establishment, to allow himself to be " *vaccinated*." He had up to that time, enjoyed a " perfect state of health ;" but immediately after he had been vaccinated he fell ill, lost the use of his right arm, never was able to sign his name afterwards, and died soon subsequently. When his life was despaired of, the " doctor" went through the usual formality of summoning another " doctor" to a " consultation," when the poor wife, out of her nearly exhausted means, had to pay a " consultation" fee exacted by that harpy " doctor," who, thus, haunted the death-bed of the poor afflicted invalid, like a vampire, to the last.

II. A specimen of a nurse.

A lady, suffering from a dangerous complaint, required the constant care of a nurse. Two nurses attended her, one by day, the other by night. When the " doctor" called to see his patient, he found that the nurse, in order to save herself trouble, had administered *double* doses of prussic acid to the helpless lady invalid, under her " charge;" whereby her patient was very nearly nursed to death.

III. A specimen of an " *undertaker*."

Quite recently an aged gentleman, (the father of the last-mentioned invalid lady,) died. The funeral was ordered, but when the body of the deceased gentleman had been placed in the coffin, supplied by the " undertaker," it was, too late, discovered that the dimensions of the coffin were inadequate, so that great force had to be used to press the poor old gentleman's body into his last over-narrow resting place. On *that* account the " undertaker" was remonstrated with, but in vain. He declared that the coffin was quite large enough, he very grossly insulted the person, (a lady,) who remonstrated against such behaviour, and, using the most violent language, declared that he would make her pay the amount agreed upon before she left his office, and frightened her into paying for the funeral before it had been performed. "Not that he wanted the money, he had plenty of his own," (he was Clerk of the Parish, gravedigger and "undertaker," coffinmaker, &c., &c., and Registrar of Births, Deaths, and Marriages), "but he would make the lady pay, at once, because she had dared to say that the coffin was too small." And this, although *that* "undertaker" knew quite well that there was no question of doubt that he would be paid in due time. This fiend in man's form must be the true tyrant-extortioner of the whole neighbourhood.

These "cases" are all supplied by *one* family, and within a brief period of time. Could one family be found, amidst millions upon millions of families in the world, in which, in the course of time, such, and far worse, instances of iniquity, tyranny, and cruelty, have *not* been experienced?

While most willingly, fully, and gratefully acknowledging all the noble work done by skilful and honourable "doctors," faithful nurses, and honest "undertakers," who, all, have to perform, at times, extremely irksome, very outwearing, or, even, revolting, services, either in behalf of suffering, or of defunct, fellow-creatures, I feel only too apprehensive lest I should have failed in giving sufficient colour to the faint picture, which I have endeavoured to submit to public view, of the before-mentioned defects, shortcomings, &c., of persons who occupy themselves in those three "businesses."

Next to the services of the sailor and of the soldier—who offer their *lives* in order to maintain our national freedom, and to secure us from the possibility of foreign tyranny—of all the services which human beings can undertake to perform, indispensable for their fellow-creatures, the "doctors," the nurses, and the "undertakers," take the *very foremost* place—none other are so honourable, because none are so *self-denying* — provided that those services are honourably, and honestly performed. With *this* proviso, no public services whatever are more deserving of *adequate*, and *certain* terms of remuneration by arrangement with the Government, than the respective services of "doctors," of nurses, and of "undertakers."

Earlsbury Park,   HENRY CLINTON.
near Royston, Herts.,
31st July, 1879.

ONE OF THE "COMMON THINGS" WHICH OUGHT TO BE UNIVERSALLY MADE KNOWN.

No. 7.

Was it not Edmund Burke who declared it useless to lay an indictment against a whole nation?

There is, however, *one* indictment which must be allowed to stand good against every semi-civilised nation on the globe, viz., the charge of *manslaughter by neglect*, in every case, *whensoever*, and *wheresoever*, death may be assumed to have ensued from deficiency in the supply of timely medical, or surgical, attendance, in cases of need.

I venture to express the hope, which I must allow myself to entertain, that the efforts which I have been making in these letters may not have been altogether lost—efforts, to show how *absolutely necessary* it is that the Government should take in hand the due consideration of this most important subject.

The populations of *towns*, however imperfectly secured they may happen to be, from *absolute* want of proper medical attendance, are, at any rate, comparatively well cared for. Those persons, on the other hand, whether high or low, rich or poor, who dwell in villages, and country places, are constantly left in a most forlorn condition, and, as far as medical services are concerned, in a most shamefully neglected state.

In the year 1817 Princess Charlotte of Wales was left by one of the foremost medical men of those days to die, for want of ordinary proper attendance. Not very long since, the young wife of a farm labourer was neglected, under precisely similar circumstances, by a very worthy country "doctor"—who resided in a town five miles away—and who had undertaken too heavy a task (in his extensive practice) to permit him to perform his duty, so as to save the life of his unlucky country patient. The poor creature, through that same doctor's negligence, lost her life.

Surely, things similar must occur, from time to time, in almost every locality, in *country* districts throughout the whole of the English Empire. Will no one, then, join with me in denouncing so crying a scandal, and in declaring that such a neglect of duty towards each other shall be made to cease?

In some of my previous letters I have endeavoured to show the way in which such glaring deficiencies might be supplied. Here, again, do I express the fervent hope, to which I hold fast, that the appeal on behalf of suffering humanity which I have ventured to submit to public consideration may not have been made, altogether, in vain.

I have spoken of "doctors," of nurses, and of "undertakers," but I have said nothing yet of sextons nor of churchyards. Little argument, however, is needed to show the degradation which accrues to the Church by retaining her hold on the office of sexton, and by her contaminating connection with burial-grounds, and cemetery companies.

How has it come to pass that the clergy, who have always, more or less, neglected the care of the *bodies* (in favour of the *souls*) of their parishoners, should have presumed that *their* care of the human *body* of the deceased parishoner should commence at *that very* period of time, when their care of the human *soul* had just passed away, out of their hands, for ever?

The shortsightedness of the Priesthood which has, everywhere, prevailed, during all these centuries, is most surprising.

Had the priests, *really*, wished well to the *souls* of their parishoners, should not their *first* care have been to look closely to the preservation of the health of their *bodies*; foreseeing (as they very well might have done) that, just for so long as they kept the *bodies* of their "clients" in health, and in life, they would still retain a hold upon the "cure" of their *souls*, which hold must cease so soon as the breath of life has quitted the body?

Moreover, had the functions of the *two* offices, viz., that of the Physician, and that of the Priest (or Schoolmaster) been *conjointly* undertaken, and honestly performed, throughout all the past centuries of Christendom, who can doubt that life would have, often, been considerably prolonged, innumerable attacks of disease averted, or infinite sufferings

alleviated; while, to the "cure" of souls, longer
time vouchsafed might have afforded so much greater
chance for the "saving" of souls?

On the other hand, is it not appalling to think of
Clergymen, *reverend* gentlemen, of all ranks, grown
fat by the continual "barter and sale," in the course
of a thousand years, of ground for burial in their
churchyards, to a constant succession of crops raised
upon the corpses of their own deceased flock? How
iniquitous, again, that clause in the regulations
of "Cemetery Companies," which enacts that all
property in a grave, *bought* and *paid for*, as a *free-
hold for ever*, shall cease, and become forfeited to
the Company, upon some paltry pretence or, even,
upon any pretence whatever!

"Jocky of Norfolk be not too bold,
For Dickon, thy master, is bought and sold."

In the present case "John Bull" stands in the
position of the master who is "bought and sold"—
not indeed, as history relates, in the original case of
Richard III., by a treacherous step-father and step-
brother—but by the treacherous, false, and grossly
partial system of representation of the people in
Parliament, and by the assumedly independent press,
too often ready to stifle public opinion, or to prevent
the "*vox populi*" from being heard any farther than
their own puny interests could permit. Were not
public opinion "under the thumb" of the public
press, we should see denounced, and crushed, for ever,
that system of sham government, resulting in the
natural consequence, that, instead of the government carrying out that which happens to be suggested,
it rather raises the question, *how* can we best shirk the
doing of that which is clearly, and conscientiously,
our duty?

"Their prime evolution
Is circumlocution—
How best to do nothing at all."

The inward conviction of "John Bull" formu-
lated in a tangible manifesto of public opinion, such
as might have been formed by good, ripe sense,
ought to make him his own master of the situation.

Instead of *this* being the case, such anarchy exists
in matters of public opinion, that the stream of
public opinion fails continually to flow down upon
its object with the irresistible power which it ought
to possess.

A great deal of quite needful objection has, for
many years, been urged against the "barter and
sale" of "church livings;" but who has ever

thought of complaining of the way in which "John Bull" has been continuously "bought and sold" in the sale of the "good-will" of "businesses" and shops, especially of "doctors" businesses, and shops, of chemists and druggists' shops, and of all other shops wherever eatable and drinkable articles are provided; in which a far more dangerous and reprehensible system of "buying and selling" has long been prevalent?

Out of the eight "branches of society," enumerated in No. 5 of these letters, the members of four of them only can be said to fulfil the duties appertaining to their respective departments, viz. :—

The Civilian......
The Producer ... these really do protect society each in
The Sailor ...... his own way.
The Soldier ......

While—
The "Doctor "......does *not* protect from Ill-health ;
The Lawyer ....does *not* protect from Injustice ;
The Merchant ......does *not* protect from Extortion ;
The Teacher ....does *not* protect from Ignorance ;

or, at least, the members of these latter four "branches of society" do not, at all, act up to the "Profession" which each of them ought to be proud to uphold the honour of.

Now, I have only one more question to ask.

The four chief evils incidental to domestic life are—

Ill-health,
Ignorance,
Injustice,
Extortion in commerce.

People who respectively offer to relieve us from the above-mentioned evils, ought, surely, to be looked upon as our best friends. They ought to be liberally provided for, and remunerated, according to the results of the good services which they perform for the benefit of the community.

But the facts are *not* so nicely adjusted as they might be, and as they ought to be, in these respects. On the contrary—almost everything, in the various departments referred to above, is left to chance-management, whilst the members of these four Departments (or Branches of Society) are left to pursue a life of precarious maintenance, for themselves, and, in many cases, for their families, just as they are allowed to pursue their own haphazard method of performing towards Society various duties, which their respective Professions ought to *require* them to perform, and ought, as far as possible, to *compel* them to perform, in the most conscientious manner.

And some of these people are of the people who, according to Mr. Gladstone's "*Savage Club*" Dinner Speech, "enjoy the privilege of creating fortunes for themselves and for their descendants."

Against a doctrine of this kind I must enter my protest, as one exceedingly unwholesome to Society. I venture to assert that, while the members of these four Professions ought to be liberally maintained as long as they continue to perform their duties towards Society—it ought to be utterly impossible that, *in the way of their respective Professions*, "fortunes" should be created, by these people, out of the very *misfortunes*, one might say, of the rest of the community.

Whatever *can best be done* under the superintendence of Government *ought to be placed* under the control of Government.

Wherever the interests and the well-being of Society are concerned, nothing should be left to blind chance or to personal whim, where, by timely foresight, it can be arranged and provided for.

In these letters I have chiefly to deal with the Department of the "Doctors," and especially in so far as their function may be assumed to embrace the efficient protection from *ill*-health of all persons committed to their charge.

As I am anxious to show *how* the thing, which is needed to be done, may *best* be done, I proceed to quote the two lines of the witless jest against the Scotch of the early part of the last century:—

"God bless his Grace the Duke of Argyle,
For setting a stone at every mile."

And to another Scottish Duke is, just now, presented a glorious opportunity, if, in his position of President of the Council of Education, his Grace the Duke of Richmond and Gordon* would like to "make his mark" in the history of humanity, and of his own age; indeed such a mark as he could effect by no other possible means.

We need now, indeed, no longer to ask to have a "*stone* placed at every mile;" but, at every mile almost in every locality—wherever requisite—we do want

---

* All the world knows that the new work, thus, proposed to be cut out for his Grace, belongs, *by routine*, to the "Home" Secretary, Mr. Cross; but, as the President of the Council may be looked upon as a comparatively "idle man," His Grace might well take the proposed additional weight off the shoulders of his already overburthened colleague.

a "dispensary" to be established, attended by at least one experienced "doctor," and a sufficient number of nurses, for the purpose of supplying timely medical and surgical advice and appliances, medicine and attendance to all persons, in the immediate vicinity, needing them. In order to effect this, all that has to be done is, that the Government should covenant with a sufficient number of "doctors," and nurses, to perform the duties required of them, at such different stations ; on condition of liberal remuneration, for all their services: in other terms—the Government should extend the body of Naval, Military, and Civil "doctors" and nurses, already paid *salaries* by Government, in various directions, and localities, so as *eventually* to embrace the whole existing medical, surgical, and obstetrical Body of Practitioners, and thus to supersede all claims for payment by "*fees*," on any account, from any body.

One other argument in favour of a system of "doctors"—paid by *fixed* salaries—as far preferable to the system of "doctors" paid by *uncertain* "fees"—I would venture to suggest: that, while we constantly hear complaints against many of the *latter* class of professional "doctors," it is comparatively rarely that the world has occasion to be shocked by charges preferred against "doctors" of the Navy, of the Army, or against "doctors" attached to Hospitals and other "doctors" paid by *fixed salaries*. And *this* seems to me to be the very best proof which could be adduced to demonstrate the absolute necessity that "doctors," and the whole of the members proposed to be attached to *their* corporate body—previously enumerated—should be made responsible to the Government for their conduct in their respective departments. In so far as every member of such a body *could be made* responsible, every such member *ought to be made* so responsible.

Earlsbury Park,   HENRY CLINTON.
Barkway, near Royston, Herts.,
1st Sept, 1879.

ROYSTON PRESS: JOHN WARREN.

ONE OF THE "COMMON THINGS" WHICH OUGHT TO BE UNIVERSALLY MADE KNOWN.

No. 8.

After the letters (Nos. 1 and 2) of this series, *signed with my own name*—had been published, in 1872, in the *Eastern Post*, two letters, from an *anonymous* correspondent, appeared, in subsequent numbers of that paper.

These letters were evidently intended, by their author, to be written, in behalf of, and in defence of the "doctors," in severe retort, antagonistic to the statements which I had made in the *Eastern Post*.

What follows was a reply made by me to that gentleman's two letters, but my reply was not printed at the time—in 1872—because the Editor evinced some reluctance to allow it to appear in his paper.

"To the Editor of the Eastern Post."

Sir,—The letter of your *anonymous* correspondent, published in your issues of the 30th and 31st of March, 1872, had the heading of

"De Bello Medicorum."

Will you permit me to suggest that a more appropriate heading for that letter would have been

"De opprobrio Medicinæ?"

Your persistently *anonymous* correspondent has, apparently from the very first, misapprehended the purpose of the statements made by me, from time to time, in the columns of the *Eastern Post*.

The objects I *had* in writing, as I have written, were—

I. To draw public attention to some of the *general* defects, and deficiencies, of the medical system.

II. To offer one or two scraps of information, which I considered, more or less, valuable to all persons; and which the experience of a lifetime, of over seventy years, had enabled me to gather.

Nobody, who will take the trouble of looking attentively over what I had written, on these subjects, can, I think, hold the opinion that anything, said by me, in those letters, could have given *reasonable* cause for the insulting, and overbearing, tone which pervades your *anonymous* correspondent's letters.

I should not make use of such severe terms on this occasion, if your correspondent had not so recklessly, and so scornfully, rejected the at least well intentioned "message of peace," with which I answered the *first*

letter he addressed to you; and if he had not dipped
his pen *again*, and *still deeper*, into the venom of
ridicule; apparently, with the heroic resolve, of
overwhelming me by that means, and of, thus,
thwarting my, really, very humble efforts towards the
relief of our suffering fellow-creatures, who are left
not so sufficiently protected, *in general*, by the medical
profession as I consider they ought to be.

I venture to state *this* as respectfully as possible.

But, as this misapprehension of my intent has
become manifest, perhaps I may be permitted to
declare, very distinctly, that my intention, when
taking a pen in hand to write on these subjects,
was originally, in no degree inspired by hostile feelings
towards any individual member of the medical profession.

Are not the members of this profession, generally
speaking, our best friends? And, if even, here
and there, in some instances, bad may happen to
be the best (within reach), is it not, always, best, and
wisest, to "make the best of a bad matter?"

"The sweeping charges, which" your correspondent so over-readily, and so unjustly, assumes
that I "make against the doctors," are, *really*, no
charges, at all, made against the doctors *individually*.

What this gentleman is pleased to call "sweeping
charges" might, much more fitly, be termed—*indications*—pointing to the general, to the, almost, uni-
versal, dissatisfaction which the present "medical
system" *must*, always, be liable to occasion, so long
as that system continues to tolerate the prevailing
very objectionable custom of accepting *fees* in remuneration for the rendering of medical service.

Your correspondent ought not to be left to sup-
pose, for one moment, that any "denunciations,"
which may have been made by me, are, really, in the
slightest degree "too ridiculous to be treated *au
sérieux*."

"The sweeping charges," made by me (not, indeed,
against the "doctors," but) against the generally existing "medical system," could be proved (if it should
be required) without any difficulty—"charges which
if proved would" not, indeed, "render them" (the
doctors) "as a body, infamous;"—but, *it is*
to be hoped, would thoroughly expose the infamy
of the generally existing "medical system," and,
thus, sooner or later, tend to secure the correc-
tion of *what* may be proved to be *evil* in that
system.

Hoping to be permitted to avail myself of your

future kind indulgence, Mr. Editor, I will reserve what I have further to say, on this extremely important subject, for another occasion: and I, now, propose to offer the only quite appropriate answer to the remaining part of your correspondent's *second* letter by requesting you to allow me to place in parallel columns the two statements made, respectively, by your correspondent, and by me.

I wish only to premise one word.

In writing what I have written in No. 1 and No. 2, "Common Things," I venture very humbly, to compare *my* action—in endeavouring to spread abroad useful knowledge — to the action of the man who sowed, in his field, good seed; while the action of your correspondent — in writing to refute what I had said—I denounce as meriting to be classed with the action of the enemy, who spitefully sowed "tares" amongst the "wheat."

In the *Eastern Post* of the 20th and 21st of Jan. last (1872), I ventured to say—"In defiance of the assurance of all those doctors who still declare that diseases *cannot be prevented*, I, on the contrary, declare my belief that Coughs, Sore-throats, Diphtheria, Laryngitis, Bronchitis, and Consumption, &c., *may often be prevented* by taking a *timely* and proper quantity of the *Camphor Julep*,* (prescribed to me many years since — to cure a hoarseness — by the late Dr. James Copland, the author of the Dictionary of Medicine).

I ventured, moreover, to say—If people wish to protect the throat, and the chest, from the attacks of diseases of many kinds, they will take from one teaspoonful to half a wineglassful of the said *Camphor Julep* as often as any feeling of uneasi-

In the *Eastern Post* of the 16th and 17th of March last (1872), your *anonymous* correspondent (who, in another letter, announced himself as a doctor,) taking for his motto—"Let the cobbler stick to his last "—sneered at me for " puffing a harmless nostrum (of the chip in porridge order.")

In the *Eastern Post* of the 30th and 31st of March (1872), the same gentleman (apparently quite forgetting the virulent, and, of course, somewhat vulgar, attack which he had, just previously, made upon the prescription in question), said, he "did not attack the marvellous *Camphor Julep* because it is, in point of fact, nothing more than a harmless saline mixture. . . ." "I venture to say, further, that anyone, who depends on it, as a means of averting the probable consequences of exposure to cold

* CAMPHOR JULEP, of the late Dr. James Copland. To protect the throat and lungs from the effects of cold, &c.

 4 oz. Camphor Water.
 1½ oz. Spirit of Minderer
 ⅓ oz. Sweet Spirit of Nitre
 ⅓ oz. Ipecacuanha Wine
 2 oz. Simple Syrup.

ness in the throat oc-
curs; and, as a safe-
guard to the *throat* and to
the *chest*, especially during
the night, they will take *at
least* one teaspoonful of
this *Camphor Julep* the
last thing at night.

Long experience (up-
wards of thirty years) induces me to believe that
even one teaspoonful of
this *Camphor Julep (if it
is only taken in time,)*
will often suffice to keep
the throat, and the chest,
free from liability to the
attacks of disease, during
the whole night, and during
even longer periods of time.

N.B. This is rather a
coarse way of asserting
that his opponent is not to
be regarded at all; while
he, (your *anonymous* correspondent, who dares not
put his name to what he
writes,) the regular prac-
titioner—is "an angel."

In a letter published in
the *Eastern Post*, I had,
likewise, ventured to assert
that the *timely*, and proper,
taking of even a *Seidlitz
Powder*, or of "Citrate of
Magnesia,") the *first thing*
in the morning, occasion-
ally, whenever requisite,
might prevent obstructions
in the intestines, in many
instances; and, thus, serve
to avert a large amount
of sufferings from disease,
—to postpone a consider-
able number of premature
deaths.

This piece of good advice
reminds us that both tea
and coffee have been ac-
cused of being poisonous.
Fontenelle lived up to
nearly his 100th birthday,
and being somewhat re-
duced in health, was told
that he should not take
coffee. "It was a poison."
But "such a slow one,"
said the philosopher.

and wet (viz.: catarrh, in
some form), will lean upon
a broken reed."

"*That* is not within the
resources of medicine.
There is no medicine, or
combination of medicines,
in the *materia medica* capable of working such a
miracle. The result of an
attempt even to modify
such consequences, would
be doubtful.

"The empiric rushes
in where the regular prac-
titioner fears to tread."

In the *Eastern Post* of
the 16th and 17th of March
(1872), your *anonymous*
correspondent said—
"When his vaulting am-
bition leads him into
the exalted region of *Seidlitz Powders* he becomes
mischievous, and it is time
to interfere."

And, then, he proceeded
to denounce the use of
Seidlitz Powders as "very
harmful." And, in a
second letter, he assured
us that "the occasional
use of *Seidlitz Powders*
and medicines of that
description is not nearly so
harmless as is popularly
supposed."

The " doctors " declare—

In Latin.	*In plain English.*
Morbos avertere !—Talem	Avert disease !—
Modum operandi — igno-	
ramus.	Such a notion we ignore.
Morbos avertere !—	To avert disease—
Nolumus.	We are *un*willing.
Id est—	That is to say—
Morbos avertere—	Avert disease—
Non *volumus.*	We *will* not,
Ergo—	Therefore—
Morbos avertere—	Avert disease—
Non *possumus.*	We *cannot.*

Earlsbury Park,   HENRY CLINTON.
   near Royston, Herts.,
   5th April, 1872.

———

P.S. in 1879.—For the plea of the " doctors " *is
verse,* I am indebted to the kind favour of a friend.

Pray, why should we *avert* disease,
And, thus, cut off our hope of fees ?
If doctors kept the land in health,
Pray whence would come the doctors' wealth ?

If men will make it worth our while,
We'll soon make this a healthier isle ;
But, in the meantime, what's the use
Of killing off the *golden goose* ?

20th *Nov.,* 1879.   ALEXANDER HUME.

———
ROYSTON PRESS : JOHN WARREN.

LaVergne, TN USA
23 December 2009
167979LV00004B